Hippopotamus means river horse. The hippo is a distant relative of the pig.

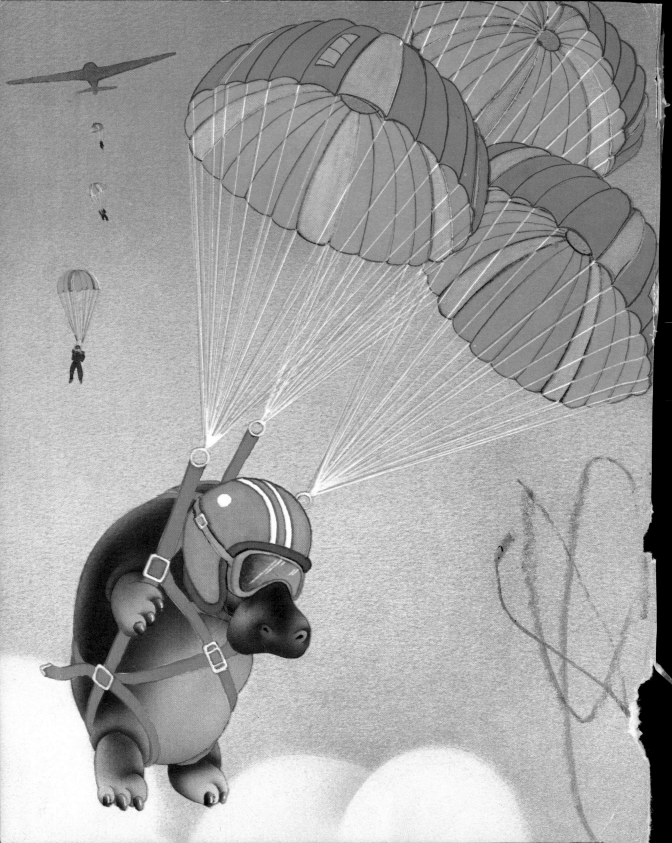

Among land animals, only an
elephant is heavier than a hippo.

The hippo spends most of its day
under water. It raises only its eyes,
ears and nose above water while
sleeping lazily.

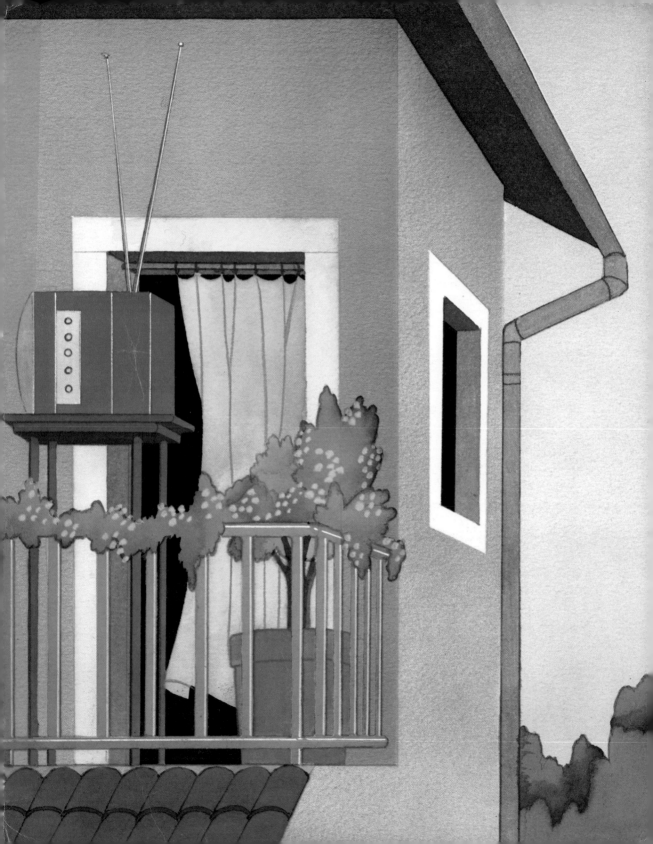

The hippo goes out at night to
search for food. It must eat
lots of grass.

Hippos can walk on the river
bottom for several minutes.

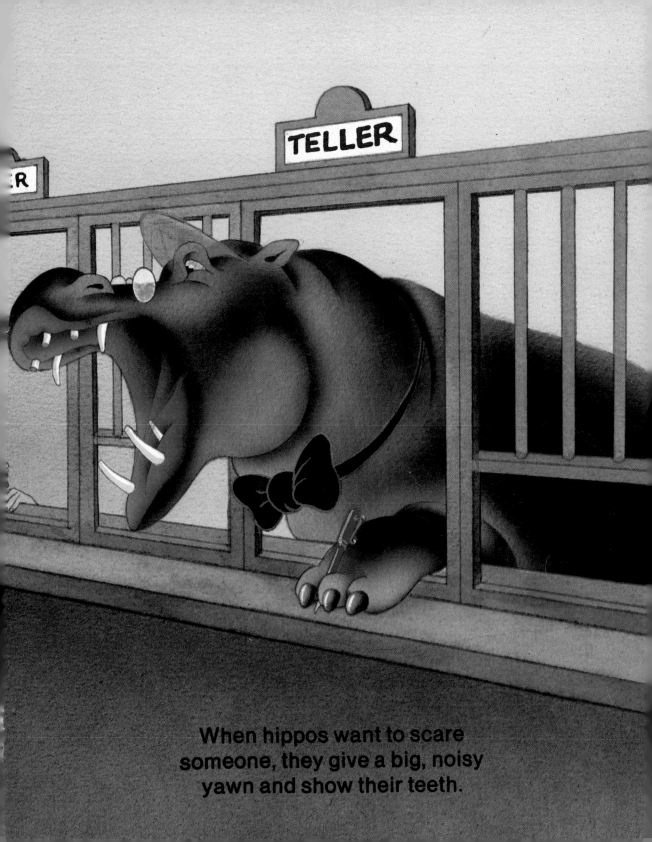

When hippos want to scare
someone, they give a big, noisy
yawn and show their teeth.

The hippo looks for shade as soon as it leaves water. The sun will quickly dry and crack its skin.

Young hippos gather to play
away from adults and babies.

Adult hippos sometimes fight
fiercely with each other, but
their wounds heal quickly.

Baby hippos can swim within minutes after they are born.